S0-BRC-935

Dear Parent,

In <u>Why Do Animals Sleep Through Winter?</u> your child will learn what it means to hibernate. Woodchuck tells about what he does to get ready for winter and why he hibernates. Turn the page and get ready for a long winter's nap.

Sincerely,

Rita D. Gould

Managing Editor

FAMILY FUN

- Talk with your child about things people do to prepare for winter—insulate windows and doors, turn on the heat in their homes, take jackets and warm clothing out of storage.

- Divide a sheet of paper into two columns. Have your child draw the sun at the top of one column. Then have your child draw snowflakes or an icicle at the top of the second column. Help your child list warm-and-cold weather activities and holidays beneath the appropriate weather symbol.

READ MORE ABOUT IT

- *What Are Seasons?*
- *Why Do Birds Fly South?*

This book is a presentation of Weekly Reader
Books. Weekly Reader Books offers book
clubs for children from preschool through high
school. For further information write to:
WEEKLY READER BOOKS, 4343 Equity Drive,
Columbus, Ohio 43228

This edition is published by arrangement
with Checkerboard Press.

Weekly Reader is a federally registered trademark
of Field Publications.

WEEKLY READER BOOKS presents

Why Do Animals Sleep Through Winter?

A **Just Ask**™ Book

Hi, my name is Christopher!

by Chris Arvetis
and Carole Palmer

illustrated by
James Buckley

FIELD PUBLICATIONS
MIDDLETOWN, CT.

During the winter, some animals hibernate.

That means they go to sleep for a long time.

The animals do this to protect themselves from the cold.

Once I get everything
ready, I go to sleep.
I wake up once in awhile.
But I don't get up until spring.
The warm weather lets me know
it's time to rise and shine.

Now you know what I do.
Let me tell you why I do it.
It is too cold in the winter.
I have no way to keep warm.
The ground is covered with
snow, so I cannot find food.

That's why I go to sleep.
When I curl up in my nest,
I stay very still.
My body cools down like
the cold air around me.
My heart slows down and
so does my breathing.
Your body does something
like this when you sleep.

Some animals sleep
all winter.
Turtles, snakes, frogs,
and toads do this.
They do not wake up until
the warm weather arrives
in the spring.

Other animals take many long naps over the winter months. Squirrels, hamsters, hedgehogs, and brown bats do this.

Still other animals take long naps, but wake up on warm days.
The animals hunt for food, and then they return to sleep.
Bears, skunks, chipmunks, and opossums do this.

Naps are great!

There are some butterflies and bugs that hibernate.

They spend the winter in places like barns, sheds, cellars, or trees.

The butterflies and insects can hide in small places and keep warm.

Animals hibernate to keep alive
during the cold weather.

As they sleep, the animals
lie very still.

Their hearts slow down and their
bodies cool down, too.

The animals live off the food they have stored in their bodies.

When the weather changes, the animals wake up.